This book is dedicated to all of the wonderful people who have made these cookies with me. I appreciate you more than you know.

Jim Tsakonas

Pauline & Kevin Sweetman

Mary Ann, Paul & Matt Hadnagy

Jennifer Work

Tony Sawyers

Stefania Anele

Rachel & Ali Lawless

Josh Spiceland

John Lapp

Matt Bugnaski

Abby Kramer

THANKS!

Stu Helm- Cover Design and Art (pg. 4-7, pg. 2 top, pg. 21 top & bottom, pg. 29 lower right, pg. 30 lower left, pg. 35 upper left, pg. 36 upper left, pg. 41-42).
Meghan Rolphe-Photography (cover, pg. 2 bottom center, pg. 8, pg. 21, pg. 22, pg. 25, pg. 28, pg. 30, pg, 34, pg, 35, pg. 40).

Sugar Momma's Cookies was a business that I created, owned, operated and put my heart into for 7 1/2 years in Asheville, NC. All great things must come to an end, and there is a life cycle to everything, but hopefully these delicious cookies and the love they represent can live on. This book contains all of the recipes I used in the cookie shop. I wrote this book so I could continue my dream of spreading joy through cookies. May these recipes help you to create some cherished memories. They sure helped me to create some. These are some really great recipes so please

enjoy!

Contents!

No, no, no!
Let me tell you
the story of how
cookies as we
know them came to be.
There was once a time where people did not have
access to sugar. Can you believe that? Well, the first
place in the world that figured out how to cultivate
sugar was a place called Iran. Back then in the 7th
century, it was called Persia. Well one of the first
things that the Persians made with sugar was cookies
of course.

When baking cakes, the Persians would test
the temperature of the oven with small amounts of
cake batter and these were the first cookies. They
were popular snacks because they were easy to travel
with. From Persia, cookies spread to Europe.

Secrets Revealed!

By the 14th century, cookies were a common treat all over Europe!

The word cookie came from The Dutch. The word for cake is koek. Little cake was called koekje. Koekje became cooky, and eventually cookie!

The chocolate chip cookie was invented in the 1930's. A woman named Ruth Wakefield was making cookies for guests at her Inn (Tollhouse Inn). She ran out of nuts and didn't know what to do! Ruth looked over and saw a chocolate candy bar and decided to break it up into little pieces and add it into the cookie dough.

They were a big hit!

HOLLAND
Koekie
Cooky,
Cookie

MASSACHUSETTS
The First
Cookie
Chip
Cookie

PERSIA
The First
Cookie

That is where cookies come from!

The Chocolate Chip Cookie Family!

Sugar Momma's big secret is that you can make 6 different varieties of cookies using one simple base dough. First, follow the instructions to make the base dough. Then, choose your flavor from the next two pages and add the last few ingredients.

9.

How to make the base dough!

You will need:

*3/4 cup white sugar

*3/4 cup light brown sugar
(Make sure it is packed when you measure it.)

*2 sticks of unsalted butter
(Cut it into little pieces, and make sure
it is at room temperature.)

*2 eggs

*1 tsp. pure vanilla extract

*1 tsp. baking soda

*1 tsp. salt

*2 1/2 cups of unbleached flour

10

For Chocolate Chip:
Add 2 cups of semisweet chocolate chips!

For Chocolate Chip Walnut:
Add 2 cups of semisweet chocolate chips and 1 cup of walnuts!

For Peanut Butter:
Add 2 cups of peanut butter chips and 1 cup of peanuts!

11.

For Peanut Butter Chocolate Chip: Add 1 1/4 cups of semisweet chocolate chips, 1 1/3 cups of peanut butter chips, and 1 cup of peanuts!

For the Super Cookie: Add 3/4 cup of semisweet chocolate chips, 3/4 cup of candy coated chocolate pieces, and 3/4 cup of butterscotch chips!

For White Chocolate Almond: Add 2 cups of white chocolate chips and 1 cup of sliced almonds!

Make the dough!

Add the white sugar, brown sugar, & butter into a slow mixer. When these ingredients have creamed together, add the eggs & vanilla. After this mixture is well blended, add the flour, baking soda, & salt. Then, add your final ingredients.

In order for the dough to become a lovely consistency for handling, you need to let it relax.

Put it in the refrigerator for at least a half hour. You can even let it chill for up to 3 days if you can wait that long. After the dough has chillaxed, you can start rolling it into 3 ounce balls. You can go one more optional step and freeze the dough balls on a cookie sheet before baking if you aren't already drooling. This dough freezes very well, so if you only wanted to make a few cookies at a time you can save the rest of the dough for later.

14.

Bake it up!

You can fit 6 of these giant cookie dough balls onto an ungreased cookie sheet. Bake them in a preheated oven at 320 degrees for about 15 minutes. Different ovens may vary. When the cookies are golden, take them out, cool and enjoy!

16.

Raw cookie dough is almost irresistible.

If you are planning on eating large quantities of it, try this recipe that doesn't include raw eggs that could make you sick.

You will need:

3/4 cup white sugar

3/4 cup light brown sugar

(Make sure it is packed when you measure it.)

2 sticks of unsalted butter

(Cut it into little pieces, and

make sure it is about room temperature.)

2/3 cup unsweetened applesauce

1 tsp. pure vanilla extract

1 tsp. baking soda

1 tsp salt

2 cups of unbleached flour

2 cups semisweet chocolate chips

Keep the mixer on low. Add the white sugar and the brown sugar into your mixer first. Then, add the butter piece by piece. Watch to make sure that it creams it all together, and that no little pieces of butter can be seen. This is when you add the applesauce and pure vanilla extract. Keep it mixing until it looks evenly blended. Next add the flour, salt and baking soda. As soon as it looks well mixed, add the chocolate chips.

18.

Yum!

19.

Here are 2 ideas of what you can do with raw cookie dough!

1. Try putting a dough ball on a stick, dipping it in melted chocolate, then freezing it for a frosty dough pop.

2. Make a cookie dough ice cream pizza. Flatten cookie dough into a pie plate and bake it until it is golden. After it cools, spread ice cream on top. Chop up frozen cookie dough and use it as a topping!

Fun Fruity Cookies!

Almond Date

You will need:
- *3/4 cup white sugar
- *3/4 cup light brown sugar (packed)
- *2 sticks of unsalted butter (cut into small pieces)
- *1 tsp. almond extract
- *2 eggs
- *2 1/2 cups unbleached flour
- *1 tsp. baking soda
- *1 tsp. salt
- *2 cups chopped dates
- *1 cup sliced almonds

Make the dough:
Add ingredients into a slow mixer in the following order: white sugar, brown sugar, butter. When those ingredients have mixed well, add the almond extract and eggs. After these have blended, add the flour, baking soda, and salt. Lastly, add the dates and almonds.

Bake it up!
After chilling the dough for a half hour or more, roll the dough into 3 ounce balls. Roll them into sugar before placing them on the ungreased cookie sheet. In a preheated oven, bake them for about 15 minutes at 320 degrees.

This recipe was inspired by a simple dessert my grandmother makes. Take a date and put an almond inside it, then roll it in sugar. Yum!

Banana Maple Walnut

You will need:
*2 bananas (riper is better)
*2 cups light brown sugar (packed)
*1 tsp. pure vanilla extract
*1/2 cup pure maple syrup
*2 cups unbleached flour
*1 1/2 tsp baking soda
*1 tsp. salt
*1 tsp. cinnamon
*3 cups old fashioned oats
*1 cup walnuts (coarsely chopped)

Make the dough:
Add the bananas into the mixer first to mash them well. Add the rest of the ingredients to the mixer in the following order: brown sugar, vanilla, maple syrup. When these have blended, slowly add the flour, baking soda, cinnamon, and oats. Lastly add the walnuts.

Bake it up!
This is a very sticky dough! Chill the dough for at least a half hour before rolling it into into 3 ounce balls. Roll the dough balls in sugar before placing them on the ungreased cookie sheet. In a pre-heated oven, bake for about 15 minutes at 320 degrees.

This is a delicious and comforting cookie made without using any animal products.

24.

Oatmeal Cranberry White Chocolate

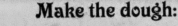

You will need:

*2 sticks of unsalted butter (cut into small pieces)
*2 cups light brown sugar (packed)
*2 tsp. pure vanilla extract
*2 eggs
*2 cups unbleached flour
*1 1/2 tsp. baking soda
*1 tsp. salt
*1 tsp. cinnamon
*3 cups old fashioned oats
*1 1/3 cup white chocolate chips
*1 1/3 cups dried cranberries

Make the dough:

Add the brown sugar & butter into a slow mixer. When blended, add the eggs & vanilla. After this blends well, add the flour, baking soda, salt & cinnamon. Then add the oats. When this is mixed well, add the white chocolate chips and cranberries. In a seperate container, make cinnamon sugar. (1 part sugar: 1/4 part cinnamon.)

Bake it up!

Chilling this dough is optional. Roll dough into 3 oz. balls and sprinkle them with cinnamon sugar. In a preheated oven, bake for about 15 minutes at 320 degrees.

Sweet, tangy, & hearty, this cookie will brighten your day!

25.

Tropical

You will need:

*2 sticks unsalted butter (cut into small pieces)
*3/4 cup white sugar
*3/4 cup light brown sugar (packed)
*1 tsp. coconut extract
*1 egg
*1 banana (the riper the better)
*2 1/2 cups unbleached flour
*1 tsp. baking soda
*1 tsp. salt
*2 cups chopped, dried pineapple
*2 cups sweetened flaked coconut

Make the dough:

Add the sugars and butter into a slow mixer. Then add the egg, coconut extract & banana. After this is blended, slowly add the flour, baking soda & salt. The last ingredients added to the mixer are the pineapple and coconut.

Bake it up!

Chill the dough for at least a half hour, then roll it into 3 oz. balls. In a preheated oven, bake them for about 15 minutes at 320 degrees.

This is a great cookie to make in the summertime, or when you want it to feel like the summer. Tropical cookie, take me away!

26.

Appledoodle

You will need:

- *2 sticks of unsalted buter (cut into small pieces)
- *1 1/2 cups white sugar
- *1 tsp. pure vanilla extract
- *1 egg
- *3 cups unbleached flour
- *1 tsp. baking soda
- *1/2 tsp. baking powder
- *3 tsp. cinnamon
- *2 cups chopped dried apples

Make the dough:

Cream the sugar and butter in a slow mixer. Add the vanilla and egg. After this is mixed, slowly add the flour, baking soda, baking powder & cinnamon. Then add the apples. In a separate container make cinnamon sugar. (1 part sugar: 1/4 part cinnamon.)

Bake it up!

Chilling this dough is optional. Roll the dough into 3 oz. balls and sprinkle with cinnamon sugar. In a preheated oven, bake for about 15 minutes at 320 degrees.

This cookie tastes like a cross between a snickerdoodle and apple pie.

27.

Holiday Cookies!

Pumpkin Chocolate Chip

You will need:

*3 sticks unsalted butter (cut into small pieces)
*2 cups light brown sugar (packed)
*1 cup white sugar
*1 egg
*1 tsp. pure vanilla extract
*1 16 oz. can of pumpkin
*4 cups unbleached flour
*2 cups old fashioned oats
*2 tsp. baking soda
*2 1/2 tsp. cinnamon
*1 tsp. salt
*1 1/4 tsp. ground ginger
* 1/2 tsp. cloves
*1 cup semisweet chocolate chips

Make the dough:

Add the brown sugar, white sugar and butter into the mixer and blend well. Then add the egg, vanilla, & pumpkin. Make sure this gets mixed very well. Then slowly add the flour, oats, baking soda, cinnamon, salt, ginger & cloves. When this is combined, then add the chocolate chips.

Bake it up!

This is a soft dough and will need to chill for at least a half hour before baking. Roll dough into 3 oz. balls and bake in a preheated oven at 320 degrees for about 15-20 minutes.

As a child, this was my birthday cookie. This is a moist and cake-like cookie. It is delicious with a schmear of peanut butter on it.

29.

Gingerbread

You willl need:

*1 1/2 sticks unsalted butter (cut into small pieces)
*1 cup sugar
*1 egg
*1/4 cup molasses
*2 1/4 cups unbleached flour
*2 tsp. ground ginger
*3/4 tsp. cinnamon
*1 tsp. baking soda
*1/2 tsp. cloves
*1/4 tsp. salt
*small bowl of sugar

Make the dough:

Cream the sugar and butter in your mixer. Add the egg and molasses to the mixer and blend well. Then add the flour, ginger, cinnamon, baking soda, cloves, & salt.

Bake it up!

Chill the dough for at least a half hour and then roll it into 3 oz. balls. Roll the dough balls in sugar and place them on the ungreased cookie sheet. Bake in a preheated oven at 320 degrees for about 15 minutes.

What a delicious wintery cookie this is! Try one with a chai tea.

Irish Soda Bread Cookie

You will need:

*1/4 cup white sugar
*1 stick butter (cut into small pieces)
*1/4 cup buttermilk
*1 egg
*2 cups unbleached flour
*1/2 tsp. baking soda
*1/4 tsp. salt
*1 tsp. caraway seeds
*1/2 cup currants or raisins

Make the dough:

Add ingredients to a slow mixer in the following order until they are blended well: sugar, butter, buttermilk, & egg. Next, slowly add the flour, baking soda, salt & caraway seeds. At the very end, add the currants or raisins.

Bake it up!

Chill the dough for at least a half hour. Roll the dough into 3 oz. balls and place them on an ungreased cookie sheet. Bake in a preheated oven at 320 degrees for about 15 minutes.

These come out almost like scones and are perfect for St. Patrick's Day.

31.

Peppermint Crunch

You will need:

*2 sticks unsalted butter (cut into small pieces)
*1 3/4 cups white sugar
*1 egg
*1 1/4 tsp. peppermint extract
*2 3/4 cups unbleached flour
*1 tsp. baking soda
*1/2 tsp. baking powder
*1-2 crushed candy canes

Make the dough:

Combine the sugar & butter in the mixer until they are creamed together. Next, add the egg & peppermint extract. When this has blended well, add the flour, baking soda, & baking powder.

Bake it up!

Chilling this dough is optional. Roll the dough into 3 oz. balls and sprinkle the crushed candy cane on top. Place the dough balls on an ungreased cookie sheet and bake in a pre-heated oven at 320 degrees for about 15 minutes.

You can't get much more festive for the holidays than this. These cookies are perfect to leave for Santa!

Rose Sugar Cookies

You will need:

*2 sticks unsalted butter (cut into small pieces)
*1 1/2 cups white sugar
*1 egg
*5 tsp. rosewater
*2 3/4 cup unbleached flour
*1 tsp. baking soda
*1/2 tsp. baking powder
*Red food coloring and a small bowl of sugar

Make the dough:

Cream together the butter and sugar in your mixer. Add the egg and rosewater. When this is mixed together well, add the flour, baking soda, & baking powder.

In a small bowl make red sugar. Add a few drops of red food coloring to a small amount of sugar and stir it with a spoon.

Bake it up!

Use a rolling pin to flatten the dough to about a thickness of 1/4 inch. Cut out shapes in the dough using cookie cutters. I like to use a heart shaped one for Valentine's Day. Sprinkle the red sugar on top of the shapes. On an ungreased cookie sheet, bake at 320 degrees for about 15 minutes.

What a romantic cookie! Your kitchen will smell like roses and cookies.

33.

Misfit Cookies!

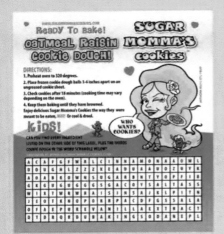

Oatmeal Raisin

You will need:

*2 sticks unsalted butter (cut into small pieces)
*2 cups light brown sugar (packed)
*1 tsp. pure vanilla extract
*2 eggs
*2 cups unbleached flour
*1 1/2 tsp. baking soda
*1 tsp. salt
*1 tsp. cinnamon
*3 cups old fashioned oats

Make the dough:

Combine the butter and brown sugar in a slow mixer. Add the vanilla & eggs. When this is thoroughly mixed, add the flour, baking soda, salt, & oats. Add the raisins last.

Bake it up!

Chilling this dough is optional. Roll the dough into 3 oz. balls. Sprinkle sugar on them before baking on an ungreased cookie sheet in a pre-heated oven at 320 degrees for about 15 minutes.

The oatmeal raisin cookie is a classic comfort food. This recipe makes a very hearty one.

35.

Sugar Cookie

You will need:
*2 sticks unsalted butter (cut into small pieces)
*1 1/2 cups white sugar
*1 tsp. pure vanilla extract
*1 egg
*2 3/4 cups unbleached flour
*1 tsp. baking soda
*1/2 tsp baking powder

Make the dough:
Cream the butter & sugar in your mixer. Add the egg & vanilla. When those ingredients are mixed well, add the flour, baking soda, & baking powder.

Bake it up!
You do not need to chill this dough. Roll the dough into 3 oz. balls and sprinkle some sugar on top. Place the dough balls on ungreased cookie sheets and bake in a preheated oven at 320 degrees for about 15 minutes.

This all occasion cookie is simple and delightful!

36.

Triple Chocolate

You will need:

*1 stick of unsalted butter
*4 ounces of baker's chocolate
*1 cup light brown sugar (packed)
*2 tsp. pure vanilla extract
*2 eggs
*1 egg yolk
*1 1/4 cup unbleached flour
*1/4 tsp. baking soda
*1/2 tsp. salt
*1 tsp. baking powder
*1/4 tsp. cloves
*3/4 cup semisweet chocolate chips
*3/4 cup white chocolate chips

If you are in the mood for chocolate, chocolate, & more chocolate, you need to try this rich cookie.

Make the dough:

In a small saucepan melt the butter and baker's chocolate on low. Stir frequently. After this has melted, add it to your mixer and slowly add the brown sugar, vanilla, eggs, & yolk. When these ingredients are mixed, add the flour, baking soda, salt, baking powder, and cloves. When all of these ingredients have mixed, then add the semisweet chocolate and white chocolate.

Bake it up!

Chill this dough for at least a half hour. Roll the dough into 3 oz. balls. Bake on an ungreased cookie sheet in a pre-heated oven at 320 degrees for about 15 minutes.

Sarsaparilla Root Beer

You will need:
*2 sticks of unsalted butter (cut into small pieces)
*1 1/4 cup sugar
*2 tbsp. molasses
*1 tsp. pure vanilla extract
*1 tsp. root beer extract
*1 tsp. sarsaparilla extract
*2 eggs
*2 1/2 cups unbleached flour
*1 tsp. baking soda
*1/2 tsp. salt

Make the dough:
Cream the butter and sugar in your mixer. Slowly add the molasses, vanilla, root beer extract, sarsaparilla extract, & eggs. When this is mixed well, add the flour, baking soda, & salt. Add the white chocolate chips last.

Bake it up!
After chilling the dough for at least a half hour, roll it into 3 oz. balls. Bake the cookies on an ungreased sheet pan. The oven should be preheated to 320 degrees. Bake for about 15 minutes.

This unique cookie is unlike any cookie you have tried before. The white chocolate is reminiscent of the foam in a root beer.

38.

Grandma's Anisette Cookies!

You will need:

*1 stick unsalted butter (cut into small pieces)
*1 cup sugar
*3 eggs
*2 tsp. anise extract
*3 cups unbleached flour
*2 tsp. baking powder
*1/2 tsp. salt

Make the dough:

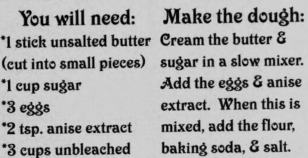

Cream the butter & sugar in a slow mixer. Add the eggs & anise extract. When this is mixed, add the flour, baking soda, & salt.

Bake it up!

Divide the dough in half and make 2 logs of dough. Flatten these logs to be about an inch thick. Place them on an ungreased cookie sheet. Bake in a preheated oven at 375 degrees for about 20 minutes. Take them out of the oven and cut one inch slices. Turn these slices on their side and bake for 10 more minutes to get them toasty.

This Italian treat can also be made with sliced almonds, mini chocolate chips, or seeds on them. Just put your topping on the logs before baking. Make Grandma proud!

There are many ways to enjoy a Sugar Momma's Cookie!

1. Grab one while it's still hot and melty. Be careful not to burn yourself.
2. Get cozy with a blanket, a movie, a glass of milk and a plate of cookies.
3. Take one along with you on a hike.
4. Have a cookie party.
5. Share cookies with a friend.
6. Make "cookie cereal." Crumble a cookie into a bowl, pour milk over it, and eat it with a spoon.
7. Make an ice cream sandwich and use cookies as the bread.
8. Substitute cookies for graham crackers in your next pudding pie.
9. Use one as a frisbee.
10. Leave cookies for all your magical entities when they come...like Santa, The Easter Bunny, or the Tooth Fairy. They work hard to bring you joy!

Made in the USA
Charleston, SC
10 October 2013